For Ryan, with love ♥ - many years too late for Mum to read to you.

Also, for boys and girls everywhere who sometimes feel lonely and want to make new friends.

ng New  Friends

Story
by
♥ Jean Janki Samaroo ♥

illustration
by
♥ Karina Garcia & Kristhiant Flores ♥

Jake and Buddy were very lonely. The two little mice wanted friends, fun, and adventure.

"I have an idea," said Jake, the short mouse. "Let's go to the cottage with our family. They go every weekend."

"How cool!" said Buddy, the tall mouse. "They won't let us go though."

Friday afternoon finally came.

Jake and Buddy hid under the fridge.

Father, Mother, Dan and Liz, were eating. Jake and Buddy could see the basket. Mother had packed crackers, cheese, jam, peanut butter, and nuts.

Jake was scared.
"That basket,"
he whispered to Buddy.

"That one," Buddy said,
pointing to the red basket.

"But wait until I say."

At the bottom of the basket, Jake and Buddy were eating. They nibbled on cheese and crackers. When they finished eating, they fell asleep.

Before long, they heard the children shouting.

"Hooray, we're here."

They could hear doors open and shut.

Father took the baskets from the trunk. In the red basket, the little mice held their breath.

They felt the thump when Father put it down.

"I can't believe we're here," Buddy said.

He crawled out of the basket. Jake was struggling to get out. Buddy reached into the basket. He grabbed Jake's hand.

Jake's head popped up. He looked around. "Our adventure has begun," he said, smiling.

After playing Cat and Mouse, Jake and Buddy scurried about everywhere.

They watched the bees, butterflies, and other insects having fun in the garden.

Soon after, they became hungry.

Time went by quickly. When it was time to leave, Chalkie and Ginger told them to come back anytime.

"Thank you," Buddy said.

"We'll look forward to that," Jake added.

They set out for the family cottage.

Chalkie and Ginger were happy to see them.

"Have you seen the movie about the lovable bear who loves honey?" Chalkie asked.

Jake and Buddy shook their heads.

"You'll like it! This movie is about him and his friends," Ginger said.

They sat close together.
They watched the movie.
After it was over, it was time to say goodbye.

Jake and Buddy were sad to leave Chalkie and Ginger.

Jake and Buddy slept in the red basket all the way home.

They were content and happy little mice. They had sweet dreams of the next week. They would go back. They would have more fun and adventure. Best of all, they would visit their new friends.

AUTHOR

Jean Janki Samaroo lives in Toronto with her husband and Ragdoll kitten, Ali. She studied Library Arts at Ryerson University and is also a Certified TESL/TEFL instructor.

Her first part-time job as a teenager was in the Children's Department of a library. In fact, most of her working life has been in libraries. Since her retirement, she's been busy taking courses, volunteering, and pursuing wholesome artistic activities.

She's always enjoyed writing and is fortunate to have the time now to express this part of herself. "Making New Friends" is her first children's story and she's delighted to be able to share it with boys and girls, parents, grandparents, librarians, and teachers everywhere.

ILLUSTRATORS

Karina Garcia and Kristhiant Flores are young and talented visual artists. They live in Toronto with their five year old son, Kyrian. They love children's books and enjoy reading and sharing stories with him. They have a keen eye for beauty and are always involved In creating projects that express this aspect of life. They are also community-minded and inspired to bring out beautiful messages for children, their families, and the communities they live in through their work.

Their artistic work includes photography, sculpture, painting, and Graphic Design — a truly multidisciplinary approach. The author was thrilled and honoured that they took on the job of illustrating this book.

About illustrating "Making New Friends," this is what they had to say. "It was one of those amazing experiences that brought a sense of adventure, imagination, and creativity, to the whole family."

MAKING NEW FRIENDS

Copyright © 2020 Jean Janki Samaroo

ISBN 978-1-7770205-1-4
All rights reserved.
The moral rights of the author have been asserted.

Story by Jean Janki Samaroo
(jeanjanki@gmail.com)

illustration by Karina Garcia & Kristhiant Flores
(karinagj.art@gmail.com)

Book Design by Kit Leung
(david_leungkit@outlook.com)